COPPERHEADS

THE SNAKE DISCOVERY LIBRARY

Sherie Bargar   Linda Johnson

Photographer/Consultant: George Van Horn

Rourke Enterprises, Inc.
Vero Beach, Florida 32964

Library of Congress Cataloging in Publication Data

Bargar, Sherie, 1944-
  Copperheads.

  (The Snake discovery library)
  Summary: An introduction to the physical
characteristics, natural environment, and
relationship to human beings of the various species
of Copperheads.
    1. Copperheads—Juvenile literature.   [1. Copper-
heads.   2. Poisonous snakes.   3. Snakes]   I. Johnson,
Linda, 1947-   II. Title.   III. Series: Bargar,
Sherie, 1944-   Snake discovery library.
QL666.069B37   1986   597.96   86-15468
ISBN 0-86592-957-2

Printed in the USA

TABLE OF CONTENTS

COPPERHEADS

One of the most common **poisonous** snakes in the eastern part of the United States is the Copperhead. The five species of Copperheads are members of the *Crotalid* family. The Copperhead gets its name from the color of its head which is like a new **copper** penny. The Copperhead has been known to live over 20 years.

Southern Copperhead
  Agkistrodon contortrix

WHERE THEY LIVE

Dry leaves, rotten logs, stone walls, wooded hills, and piles of trash are favorite hiding places of the Copperhead. Ponds, streams, or swamps are usually nearby. Copperheads live in the eastern United States and Texas. The cold, short winter days often find the Copperhead **hibernating** in dens with Timber Rattlesnakes. As the days grow warmer and longer, the Copperhead **basks** in the sun.

6

Broad-banded Copperhead
Agkistrodon laticinctus

HOW THEY LOOK

The thick Copperhead body is about 3 feet long and covered with scales. Each scale has a small ridge down the middle. Its light brown body with dark markings **camouflages** the snake in piles of dead leaves. Its head is shiny and the color of **copper**.

Broad-banded Copperhead
Agkistrodon laticinctus

THEIR SENSES

The Copperhead flicks out its tongue to pick up the scent of its **prey**. The Jacobson's organ in the roof of its mouth **analyzes** the scent to learn what is nearby. At close range, the eyes and heat receptor pits on the face of the snake give it the location and size of the **prey**. As soon as the **prey** is close enough, the Copperhead strikes.

11

Southern Copperhead
Agkistrodon contortrix

THE HEAD AND MOUTH

The Copperhead's chunky head has two heat receptor pits. Long, hollow fangs which are folded against the roof of the mouth are extended during a bite. Muscles around the **venom** glands pump the **venom** through the fangs and into the **prey**. The jaws stretch like a rubber band to swallow the animal whole. The windpipe extends from the throat to the front of the mouth and allows the snake to breathe while swallowing **prey**.

Southern Copperhead
Agkistrodon contortrix

BABY COPPERHEADS

The mother Copperhead has from 1 to 14 babies in August, September or October. The baby Copperhead is about 8 inches long and has a yellow tail. The baby sheds its skin for the first time within 10 days after its birth. The baby will be an adult in 3 years.

Baby Southern Copperhead

PREY

The famous quick strike of the Copperhead kills its **prey**. Mice, lizards, frogs, insects, and birds are the common meals of the Copperhead. The baby Copperhead wiggles its yellow tail to attract small **prey**. While the **prey** watches the tail, the snake bites the animal. The Copperhead swallows its **prey** head first. Birds, other snakes, and pigs eat Copperheads.

Southern Copperhead
   Agkistrodon contortrix

THEIR DEFENSE

Copperheads do not like to fight. **Camouflaged** in dry leaves, they lie still as an enemy comes close. If the Copperhead is disturbed, it **vibrates** its tail back and forth across the dry leaves. It sounds like the rattle of a rattlesnake. If the enemy comes too close, the Copperhead strikes.

Broad-banded Copperhead
Agkistrodon laticinctus

COPPERHEADS AND PEOPLE

The bite of the Copperhead does not often kill a person, but it does hurt. It makes the person sick and damages the tissue around the bite. The **venom** of the Copperhead is being studied by medical scientists. It may be very valuable in the study of human blood.

GLOSSARY

analyze (AN a lyze) analyzes — To find out what something is.

bask (BASK) basks — To lie in and enjoy warmth.

camouflage (CAM ou flage) camouflages, camouflaged — The color of an animal's skin matches the ground around it.

hibernate (HI ber nate) hibernating — To sleep or not be active during the winter season.

poison (POI son) poisonous — A substance that causes sickness or death when it enters the body.

prey (PREY) — An animal hunted or killed by another animal for food.

venom (VEN om) — A chemical made in animals that makes other animals and people sick or kills them.

vibrate (VI brate) vibrates — To move back and forth.

INDEX